A Spiritual Journey Of Life, Love, and Forgiveness

BY:
CAROL A. SEALES

A Spiritual Journey of
Life, Love and Forgiveness

Copyright ©2021
by Carol A. Seales

Printed in
the United States of America

Published by
Kingdom Publishing, LLC

All irght reserved. No part of
this book may be reproduced or
transmitted in any form or by any
means, electronic or mechanical,
including photocopying, recording
or by any information storage and
retrieval system without written
permission from the author.

Edited by
Christian Andrew

ISBN
978-1-947741-70-6

This book is dedicated to my Lord and Savior, Jesus Christ.

Thank you Lord for;
Life, Love and Forgiveness.

To my beautiful late Mother – my heart.
To my Dad – who was my rock.
To my brother – my friend.

To my family and friends who have passed on and who are still here.
Thank you for your support.

Love you all!

Contents

Connect 7

Vote For Jesus! 9

Mother: My Loving Angel 11

The Flesh 13

The Good News! 15

What Your Love Has Brought Me Through 17

Sunshine 19

Where Do I Belong? 21

The Body Temple 23

God Is Good! 24

Love 26

Bird Songs 29

Christ Died For Me!!!! 30

Depression 32

God's Child 35

Grace & Mercy 36

Comforter 39

Knocking On Heaven's Door 41

My Dad 43

Freedom 45

Only God! 47

Hold On! 49

The Evil One 51

Walk With God! 53

A Brother's Love 55

Peace 57

Are You Out There? 58

Connect

Lord,
Please help me to connect with life again.

I want to reach out and help someone.

I want to love again.

I feel as though I am lost; spiritually and emotionally.

My connection with life was my mother. Your love and her love
brought me through life's pain.

My heart aches for her love but I know your love will give me strength,
courage and power to overcome my trials and tribulations of life.

Vote For Jesus!

As I drive to work on this beautiful morning, I see signs on people's lawns.

It says to vote for this person, vote for that person. I understand it's election time but I have no idea of the people mentioned on those lawns. Those names mean nothing to me.

However, there is a name I do know.

A name I've known all my life.

This name I call on through the good and bad times.

This name I know loves me.

He is the truth that won't lie, trick or manipulate.

His name is Jesus.

Won't you please vote for Him.

Mother: My Loving Angel

Lord, it's been over 10 years since Mom passed on and I still shed tears for her because I miss her.

I have been blessed to have an Angel, (Mom), in my life that birthed me, fed me, clothed me and simply loved me as you love me Lord; Unconditional.

When I was young I thought a love like hers would last forever.

As I got older, I saw my angel being taken away from me and my family.

Something invaded her body. That something was cancer.

Cancer took her mind and body but did not take her spirit nor her soul.

Her spirit lives on like a cool summer breeze.

Her smile reigns on like a beautiful summer day.

When I see a butterfly, it reminds me of her.

I want to catch it and never let go.

Knowing that I'll see her again keeps me strong.

I love you Mommy.

The Flesh

LORD,
I gave into the one thing I didn't want to be.

You gave me wisdom of how not to be that person. The person that becomes weak in the flesh.

You told me through your word that you are my everything.

From Your word You taught me not to please man but to please You
with righteous living, to have a good and loving heart.

LORD,
please be patient with me, this sinner.

I know I will bounce back again because I have You to guide me and to keep me strong.

The Good News!

As I left work today, I looked up into the sky. I saw two clouds.

In the clouds, it looked as if two angels were facing each other playing trumpets.

I watched the two angels for a while. I asked myself, what could they be playing on their trumpets?

Maybe they were sounding off that God is with me.

God feels my pain.

God is my comforter.

God hears my prayers.

Now go!

Pray more, read your Bible more and help tell others the Good News so that they may have salvation also!

What Your Love Has Brought Me Through

God, your love is so Awesome. More Awesome than anything on earth.

Your love has brought me out of shame, wickedness, emotional, mental and physical pain, misery, depression, sickness, surgeries, family dispute, troubled marriage, debt, loneliness, heartache and negativity.

There are no words that I can say or no words that can measure up to thank you.

Sometimes my past won't allow me to rest. It keeps haunting me.

But when I think about how much you love me, then I'm alright again.

The only way I can give back to you is to make you proud of me.

I pray I will be able to make you proud before I enter your kingdom.

Sunshine

As I look out my apartment window on this February winter day I see clouds, bare trees and bushes.

I see cars and trucks go by. I wonder where they're going.

Could they be going shopping, to Church, hospital, movies, work or just out for a drive.

Then the Sun comes out; that beautiful yellow sun.

It shines because though we may have things to do and responsibilities to take care of, we must not forget that when it's cloudy or dark there's always Sunshine at the end of the tunnel.

Where Do I Belong?

The need to belong is so important.

God brings so many people in our lives.

Some people are bad and some are good.

How do we decide which ones to be around?

I put myself in the middle.

I want to belong and be there for everyone but that's not always the case.

You'll have those who will take advantage of you and hurt you.

There are those who want to bring you down and not see you get ahead.

Those people you stay away from.

There are people who try to look out for your wellbeing and ask for nothing in return.

Those people I gravitate to because they are more like me.

That's where I belong, with those people who look at everyone the same; as God does.

The Body Temple

We think because we are our own selves that our body belongs to us.

We abused it, torture and mistreat our body.

Some of use let any and every-one do as they please with our bodies.

We need to be strong and understand that our body is a temple and it belongs to God.

We have to be careful what we put in it and on it.

We're supposed to Treasure and cherish our Temple because God created us; not man.

God Is Good!

God is good all the time …all the time God is good!

When we cry, God is good.

When we laugh, God is good.

When we're angry, God is good.

When we're happy, God is good.

When we sin, God is good.

When we live right, God is good.

When we're lonely, God is good.

When we're in a crowd, God is good.

When we're cocky, God is good.

When we're humble, God is good.

When we're hungry, God is good.

When our bellies are full, God is good.

When we're poor, God is good.

When we're rich, God is good.

When we stumble and fall, God is good.

When we stand up, God is good.

God is ALWAYS good and is ALWAYS there for us no matter what we go through.

Love

LOVE is a powerful four letter word.

LOVE will make you feel like you're on top of the world and it can also make you feel very low.

LOVE doesn't put material things before you.

LOVE makes you feel protected and secure.

LOVE is quick to give than to take.

LOVE will nurse you back to health.

LOVE is a good listener.

LOVE won't judge you.

LOVE won't curse or hit you.

LOVE knows when you need a shoulder to cry on.

LOVE will stand up for you when others put you down.

LOVE will treat you with respect whether you are rich or poor, educated or not.

LOVE has a forgiving heart.

LOVE doesn't break promises.

LOVE removes you out of a stressful environment.

LOVE appreciates and doesn't take you for granted.

So when love comes in your life, don't abuse it , embrace it.

Bird Songs

Let us take the time to listen, listen to the songs the birds are singing.

They sing to each other for mating or for territory.

To us, they sound like songs from heaven.

Their songs seem as though they are telling us to appreciate what God has given us!

To appreciate the clouds, sun, sky, trees, the air we breathe, the morning when we rise and the night for resting.

We should appreciate all the beauty that God has given us freely.

Christ Died For Me!!!!

CHRIST DIED FOR ME!

- What have you done besides create a stressful environment for me?

CHRIST DIED FOR ME!

- What have you done besides having desires of hitting me?

CHRIST DIED FOR ME!

- What have you done besides allowing others to put me down?

CHRIST DIED FOR ME!

- What have you done besides leave me out in the cold?

CHRIST DIED FOR ME!

- What have you done besides emotionally abused me?

CHRIST DIED FOR ME!

- What have you done besides leave me when I was ill to wither up and die?

It was Christ that died on the cross for yours and my transgressions.

We should have nothing but gratitude for him.

There is no other love that would do what Christ has done for us.

No other!

Depression

Why do I feel sadness, unworthy, and weak? Tears flowing at any given moment.

I can't get out of bed and I don't want to get out of bed.

Darkness overshadows me.

This "thing" called depression is a horrible feeling.

It seems to take over my life.

It drains all the energy out of me.

My hopes and dreams seem as though I will never reach them.

Then faith steps in!

GOD's light overshadows the darkness!

GOD pours his gracious love into our hearts and minds.

No matter how much we feel alone, GOD is ALWAYS there; listening, comforting us with His gracious love.

Letting us know we are not alone.

So be not afraid, GOD tells us.

FOR HE IS THE GREAT I AM!

We are going to have hard and difficult times, some worse than others but we have to always remember we are GOD's children!

HE IS OUR ALMIGHTY FATHER!

He loves us and is always there for us no matter what we go through.

God's Child

What is the difference between a homeless person and a person that lives in a mansion?

Money, but they're still God's child.

What is the difference between a prisoner and a free man?

Circumstance, but they're still God's child.

What is the difference between a disabled person and a non-disabled person?

Disability, but they are still God's child.

What is the difference between a person from Alaska and a person from Africa?

Location, but they're still God's child.

No matter where you're from or what you go through, we are all God's children.

If we see our brethren in need and we have it to give, then share and give from the heart.

So let us not judge each other .

Only God can do that.

Grace & Mercy

Lord, there was a time when my mind was going through so much confusion.

I felt so much turmoil.

All I saw was darkness around me.

I shut myself down spiritually, emotionally, physically, and mentally.

I felt myself slipping away fast.

During that time I felt depressed.

I cried a lot and prayed a lot.

I felt you comforting me.

Telling me to hold on and that this storm shall pass!

To trust and believe!

I let all my worries and anxieties go!

The darkness turned into light!

God's Grace and Mercy saved me, healed me from my sickness of depression!

I can live and love again!

Thank you Father.

Comforter

Lord, it is amazing how comforting your love makes me feel.

When I felt myself going deeper and deeper into a dark place, a place I thought I could not return from, I had to find a way to escape.

When I finally took the time to stop, look and listen to realize;

YOU made the trees.

YOU made the sky, clouds, sun, moon and stars.

YOU make the birds sing.

YOU make the gentle breeze that flows through the trees.

Just to see a praying mantis on my window screen or a butterfly landing in my hand, it's comforting to know that you are the Creator of the world and that YOUR love is so gentile.

Knocking On Heaven's Door

Please LORD, please be there!

I'm knocking LORD, can you hear me?

I'm hurting badly.

So much pain, so much guilt, so much anger, so much anxiety!

I need you Father!

Only YOU can make it all better.

Only YOU can make the pain go away.

There is no one that can heal my heart, body, and soul but YOU.

THANK YOU LORD for opening the door, thank you for listening.

My Dad

As a child, I looked at my Dad as being strong.

I never saw a tear shed from his eyes.

He worked hard every day to provide for the family.

In his spared time, he would draw, carved wood, rode his bicycle and listened to his music, especially jazz.

I used to emulate him.

I started drawing at the age of 10 and I loved riding my yellow Italia 10-speed bike.

My Dad showed me how to be independent without actually teaching me how.

My Dad was young at heart.

He loved to give to the homeless as well as his co-workers.

His giving heart made him happy and that puts a smile on my face.

Freedom

Before the age of 18, I had a lot of confidence with a very strong-willed personality.

People always saw me as a strong person.

A person that could withstand anything.

Behind closed doors I was afraid of success because I hated to fail.

But now, I don't feel that way.

God has given me the confidence to overcome all obstacles!

When I stand on His shoulders, I feel strong!

"I can do anything through Christ who strengthens me!"

Philippians 4:13

Only God!

There will always be situations and problems that are out of our control.

You try to take on these problems but they become overwhelming.

Realizing you can't fight your battles by yourself so you fall to your knees!

You cry and pray, pray and cry to GOD to help you.

Once you let go and let GOD, you start seeing the battle is not yours, it's the Lord's!

Only GOD makes things right in His time!

Hold On!

Life is full of surprises.

Life is full of ups and downs.

One day you're enjoying all that is good in life.

The next day, you might be experiencing a very traumatic situation in your life and questioning … why me?

Circumstances happen and will always happen in life.

We have to remember to hold on and stand strong. Our faith and trust in GOD will make everything alright again.

Hold on and don't give up!

GOD is with you!

You just have to believe.

The Evil One

There are times when you feel alone.

You feel as though people in your family, on your job or in school that are against you, attacking you.

Reasons being, you feel as though you don't fit in or you might not agree with the negativity that's surrounding you, which involves your family or friends.

There is a possibility someone has bullied you and brought you to tears.

The evil one constantly wants to see you fail.

The evil one wants to make you feel sorry for yourself no matter what you do.

The evil one sits back with an evil grin just waiting for us to destroy our lives.

However, there is someone who is more powerful than the evil one.

Someone who will take you by your hand and take you from darkness and bring you into His glorious light!

GOD is forever our protector!

GOD is forever our provider!

GOD is forever faithful and merciful!

Walk With God!

There is a lovely couple I know who love each other dearly.

The husband was diagnosed with colon cancer and it is metastasizing to his organs a little at a time.

However, he does not appear to have this horrible illness. The doctors are saying the x-rays and scans should contribute to tremendous pain.

This man has tremendous faith in God the Father.

His response to the doctors: "I WALK WITH GOD!"

You see, this man knows GOD and by knowing Him, he can live and still praise God's Holy name through any circumstances that comes his way.

He and his wife are truly angels because they both are believers in Christ.

Therefore, no adversity can come between them.

GOD is their salvation forever more!

Inspired by Alice and Douglas

A Brother's Love

I will never forget the day you were born.

I was so excited when Mom and Dad were bringing you home from the hospital.

The memories of us growing up together, playing and teasing each other.

A brother's love is one of protection, a listener, to give advice and to share problems and situations with.

A brother's love never judges you and never turns his back on you.

I will always treasure and take this love with me forever and ever!

Peace

Every day that I wake up, I give thanks to you – GOD.

I thank YOU because the body is weak during sleep.

YOU are watching over me with every breath I take and every dream I make.

YOU have a purpose for my life.

I thank YOU for getting me closer to my purpose.

Sometimes I have feelings of uneasiness and turmoil.

A feeling of worthlessness.

Sometimes my confidence turns to meekness.

However, when I say YOUR name, there is a feeling of peace.

Only YOU have the power to make the meek feel confident and for the weak to be strong!

THANK YOU JESUS!

Are You Out There?

There is a man out there in the world that I pray about.

He does not know me and I do not know him.

If our paths ever cross, I pray he will be a man who;

*Puts GOD First.

*Respects me.

*Knows he is strong mentally and physically but has a gentle and patient nature.

*Is not distracted by the things of the world.

*Has his life altogether and is secure in his own mind.

*Not full of envy or jealousy.

*Leads the crowed not follows it.

*Enjoys walks and talks on any given day.

*If he has a bad day, does not take his aggression out on me but is happy to come to me for a caress or kind word.

*Stands his ground with family, friends and associates.

*Does not manipulate or take me for granted.

*Says "don't worry .. I'll take care of it"… and does.

Final Thoughts

In January of 2007, I picked up my pen and started writing my poems because I felt the presence of GOD redirecting me away from a dark time in my life.

GOD inspired me to write, so I wrote.

GOD's love brought me through the darkness.

No matter what challenge we go through in life, GOD is always there to get us through by HIS grace, love, and mercy.

www.ingramcontent.com/pod-product-compliance
Lightning Source LLC
Chambersburg PA
CBHW081756100526
44592CB00015B/2459